Reach
Out
for Your
Dreams

Other books by

Blue Mountain Press INC

Come Into the Mountains, Dear Friend
by Susan Polis Schutz
I Want to Laugh, I Want to Cry
by Susan Polis Schutz
Peace Flows from the Sky
by Susan Polis Schutz
Someone Else to Love
by Susan Polis Schutz
I'm Not That Kind of Girl
by Susan Polis Schutz
Yours If You Ask
by Susan Polis Schutz
Love, Live and Share
by Susan Polis Schutz
Find Happiness In Everything You Do
by Susan Polis Schutz

The Language of Friendship
The Language of Love
The Language of Happiness
The Desiderata of Happiness
by Max Ehrmann
I Care About Your Happiness
by Kahlil Gibran/Mary Haskell
I Wish You Good Spaces
Gordon Lightfoot
We Are All Children Searching for Love
by Leonard Nimoy
Come Be with Me
by Leonard Nimoy
Creeds to Love and Live By
On the Wings of Friendship
You've Got a Friend
Carole King
With You There and Me Here
The Dawn of Friendship
Once Only
by jonivan
You and Me Against the World
Paul Williams
I Promise You My Love
Thank You for Being My Parents
A Mother's Love
A Friend Forever
gentle freedom, gentle courage
diane westlake
You Are Always My Friend
When We Are Apart
It's Nice to Know Someone Like You
by Peter McWilliams
These Words Are for You
by Leonard Nimoy
It Isn't Always Easy
My Sister, My Friend
Thoughts of Love
Thoughts of You, My Friend

Reach Out for Your Dreams

A collection of poems
Edited by Susan Polis Schutz

Blue Mountain Press ™

Boulder, Colorado

Library of Congress Number: 80-65752
ISBN: 0-88396-078-8

Manufactured in the United States of America
First Printing: March, 1980
Second Printing: September, 1980
Third Printing: September, 1982

Thanks to the Blue Mountain Arts creative staff, with special thanks to Faith Hamilton and Richard Schoenberger.

ACKNOWLEDGMENTS are on page 62

Blue Mountain Press INC.

Boulder, Colorado

CONTENTS

One day at a time—this is enough. Do not look back and grieve over the past, for it is gone; and do not be troubled about the future, for it has not yet come. Live in the present, and make it so beautiful that it will be worth remembering.

—Ida Scott Taylor

Hold fast to dreams
for if dreams die,
life is a broken
winged bird that
cannot fly.

—Langston Hughes

Look
to the future
and not to the past
to find
those things
you
want to
make last

—jonivan

This life is yours
Take the power
to choose what you want to do
and do it well
Take the power
to love what you want in life
and love it honestly
Take the power
to walk in the forest
and be a part of nature
Take the power
to control your own life
No one else can do it for you
Take the power
to make your life happy

—Susan Polis Schutz

Whatever the struggle
continue the climb
it may be only
one step to the summit

—diane westlake

There is only one success—
to be able to spend your life
in your own way.

—Christopher Morley

Those who bring sunshine
to the lives of others
cannot keep it from
themselves.

—Sir James Barrie

The best and most beautiful
things in the world
cannot be seen
or even touched.
They must be felt
with the heart.

—Helen Keller

There are many fine things which you mean to do some day, under what you think will be more favorable circumstances. But the only time that is surely yours is the present, hence this is the time to speak the word of appreciation and sympathy, to do the generous deed, to forgive the fault of a thoughtless friend, to sacrifice self a little more for others. Today is the day in which to express your noblest qualities of mind and heart, to do at least one worthy thing which you have long postponed, and to use your God-given abilities for the enrichment of some less fortunate fellow traveler. Today you can make your life . . . significant and worthwhile. The present is yours to do with it as you will.

—Grenville Kleiser

All things are possible to him that believeth.

—Mark 9:23

Some men see things as they are
and say, "Why?"—
I dream things that never were
and say, "Why not?"

— George Bernard Shaw

A dreamer lives for eternity

—Anonymous

TRUE GREATNESS

A man is as great as the dreams he dreams,
    As great as the love he bears;
As great as the values he redeems,
    And the happiness he shares.
A man is as great as the thoughts he thinks,
    As the worth he has attained;
As the fountains at which his spirit drinks,
    And the insight he has gained.
A man is as great as the truth he speaks,
    As great as the help he gives,
As great as the destiny he seeks,
    As great as the life he lives.

—C. E. Flynn

Live—decently, fearlessly, joyously—and don't forget that in the long run it is not the years in your life but the life in your years that counts!

—Adlai Stevenson

Do not follow where
the path may lead.
Go, instead, where there is no path
and leave a trail.

—Anonymous

It is a funny thing about life;
if you refuse to accept
anything but the best,
you very often get it.

—Somerset Maugham

Ask, and it shall be given you;
seek, and ye shall find;
knock, and it shall be opened
unto you.

—Matthew 7:7

Every morning is a fresh beginning. Every day is the world made new. Today is a new day. Today is my world made new. I have lived all my life up to this moment, to come to this day. This moment—this day—is as good as any moment in all eternity. I shall make of this day—each moment of this day—a heaven on earth. This is my day of opportunity.

—Dan Custer

Today is the first day
of your future.

—Anonymous

Keep your face to the sunshine and you cannot see the shadow.

—Helen Keller

To accomplish great things,
we must not only act,
but also dream,
not only plan,
but also believe.

—Anatole France

The grand essentials
to happiness
in this life are
something to do
something to love
and something
    to hope for.

—Joseph Addison

Always remember
to forget
the things
that made you sad,
but never forget
to remember
the things
that made you glad.

—Elbert Hubbard

There is no meaning to life
except the meaning man gives
to his life by the unfolding
of his powers.

—Erich Fromm

The people who get on in this
world are the people who get up
and look for the circumstances
they want, and, if they can't
find them, make them.

—George Bernard Shaw

It is a life of wonderment—
    enjoy—share—grow
It will be only
as you
make it.

—jonivan

Life is not a problem
to be solved,
but a reality
to be experienced.

—Soren Kierkegaard

The great thing
in this world
is not so much
where we are,
but in what direction
we are moving.

—Oliver Wendell Holmes

If one advances confidently in
the direction of his dreams,
and endeavors to live the life
which he has imagined,
he will meet with a success
unexpected in common hours.
. . . If you have built castles in the air,
your work need not be lost;
that is where they should be.
Now put foundations under them.

—Henry David Thoreau

I was taught at an early age
that you make your own life.
You make your own happiness,
your own unhappiness.
My philosophy is that
what you put out
comes back to you.
I firmly believe that.

—Cheryl Ladd

. . . I'm doing what I should have done years ago, which is finding out who I am and what I want. I want to have a choice. And when I make decisions through choice, not duty, it has to be better for me and for the people who love me and the people I love.

—Louise Fletcher

Do not wish to be anything
but what you are,
and try to be that perfectly.

—St. Francis De Sales

Life is sweet because of the
    friends we have made
And the things which in common
    we share;
We want to live on, not because
    of ourselves,
But because of the ones who
    would care.
It's living and doing for
    somebody else
On that all of life's splendor
    depends,
And the joy of it all, when we
    count it all up,
Is found in the making of friends.

—Anonymous

Far away there in the sunshine
are my highest aspirations. I may
not reach them, but I can look up
and see their beauty, believe in them,
and try to follow where they lead.

—Louisa May Alcott

You can always find
the sun within yourself
if you will only search.

—Maxwell Maltz

If you can't be a highway,
   then just be a trail,
If you can't be the sun,
   be a star,
It isn't by size that you
   win or you fail—
Be the best of whatever you are!

—Douglas Malloch

. . . I'm in touch with myself, and it feels wonderful. For the first time I don't have to prove why I'm here; I can just be. Being in touch gives you such great freedom and aliveness and love—and I want all those things to get continually more real for me.

—Valerie Harper

I may not be the fastest
I may not be the tallest
        Or the strongest

I may not be the best
Or the brightest

  But one thing I can do better
  Than anyone else . . .

        That is

          To be me

            —Leonard Nimoy

What lies behind us
and what lies before us
are tiny matters
compared to what lies within us.

—Ralph Waldo Emerson

Happiness cannot
come from without.
It must come
from within.
It is not what we
see and touch or
that which others
do for us
which makes us happy;
it is that which we
think and feel and do,
first for the other fellow
and then for ourselves.

—Helen Keller

Reach out in the early morning mist,
As the day's sun
Breaks the calmness of night,
And rise to the new day,
A new awareness of being.

Shake hands with the world,
And smile.

It's great to be alive.

—jonivan

The most wonderful
of all things in life,
I believe, is the discovery
of another human being
with whom one's relationship
has a glowing depth, beauty,
and joy as the years increase.

This inner progressiveness
of love between
two human beings
is a most marvelous thing,
it cannot be found
by looking for it or
by passionately wishing for it.
It is a sort of Divine accident.

—Sir Hugh Walpole

You are equal to all others
some may have greater
    talents and power
where you are lacking
but you are greater in areas where
    they cannot go
do not stop your own growth
    and progression
by trying to emulate . . .
or follow . . . anyone
step out with courage
develop all that you are meant to be
look for new experiences . . .
meet new people
learn to add all new dimensions
to your present and future
you are one of a kind . . .
equal to every other person
accept that fact
live it   use it   stand tall
in belief of who you are
reach for the highest accomplishment
touch it   grasp it
know it is within your ability
live to win in life
and you will

—diane westlake

ACKNOWLEDGMENTS

We gratefully acknowledge the permission granted by the following authors, publishers and authors' representatives to reprint poems and excerpts from their publications.

Ladies' Home Journal for "I'm in touch with myself," by Valerie Harper. Copyright © 1976 LHJ Publishing, Inc. Reprinted with permission of Elizabeth Kaye and LADIES' HOME JOURNAL. And for "I'm doing what I should," by Louise Fletcher. Copyright © 1977 LHJ Publishing, Inc. Reprinted with permission of Elizabeth Kaye and LADIES' HOME JOURNAL. And for "I was taught," by Cheryl Ladd. Copyright © 1979 LHJ Publishing, Inc. Reprinted with permission of Patricia Miller and LADIES' HOME JOURNAL. All rights reserved.

jonivan for "Look to the future" and "Reach out," by jonivan. Copyright © jonivan, 1978. And for "It's a life of wonderment," by jonivan. Copyright © jonivan, 1979. Reprinted by permission. All rights reserved.

International Creative Management for "I may not be the fastest," by Leonard Nimoy. Copyright © Leonard Nimoy, 1978. Reprinted by permission. All rights reserved.

Harold Ober Associates for "Hold fast to dreams," by Langston Hughes. Copyright 1932 by Langston Hughes. Renewed. Reprinted by permission. All rights reserved.

Simon & Schuster for "You can always find," by Maxwell Maltz. Copyright © 1975 by the estate of Maxwell Maltz, M.D., F.I.C.S. Reprinted by permission. All rights reserved.

Diane Westlake for "whatever the struggle," and "you are equal," by diane westlake. Copyright © diane westlake, 1978. Reprinted by permission. All rights reserved.

A careful effort has been made to trace the ownership of poems used in this anthology in order to get permission to reprint copyrighted poems and to give proper credit to the copyright owners.

If any error or omission has occurred, it is completely inadvertent, and we would like to correct it in future editions provided that written notification is made to the publisher: BLUE MOUNTAIN PRESS, INC., P.O. Box 4549, Boulder, Colorado 80306